The Budget Cookbook
For Brunches, Buffets and Cocktail Parties

by Dorothy Neiswender Kent
and Martha Alcott Dessem

Illustrated by Phyllis Benjamin

Published in Association with *Parade Magazine*

Grosset & Dunlap
A National General Company
Publishers   New York

Contents

Introduction   5

Planning The Party   7

Brunches For Six   9

Buffet Dinners For Twelve   27

Cocktail Parties For Fifteen   57

Desserts   80

Beverages   88

Index   93

Introduction

Good appetite and the joy of entertaining friends are undoubtedly two of life's great pleasures. The anticipation of a party not only adds zest to living before the event, but affords pleasure during it for the hosts as well as the guests. However, many times the zest is diminished by attendant anxieties!

What to serve? How much of everything do I need? How much will it cost? Can we afford it? Too often the special brunch, the informal or formal cocktail party, the dinner doubly owed to friends, is postponed because the anxieties outweigh the desire, or cloud the need to fulfill the obligation.

The purpose of this book is to help you plan your party; know what to buy; how much it will cost; and, probably most important of all, how to achieve ease in serving, as well as in the preparation and cooking of the entire menu.

In assembling the ingredients for each menu "price-wise" there has been no compromise with quality and no compromise with amounts to give each guest comforting sustenance. And, "time-wise" so many things can be done ahead of time. Copy down your shopping list. Check your condiments and staples. Shop well ahead of time. Then prepare, when suggested, many of the dishes, sauces, and spreads hours ahead of time, or even several days before the party.

So, to the appreciative adherents of good food and good company, it is hoped that this book will pave your way to good appetite, pleasurable concourse with friends, and a surcease of anxiety!

Dorothy Neiswender Kent
Martha Alcott Dessem

Planning the Party

The wise hostess avoids inviting too many guests to a party. Following a menu and the number it will include will aid the hostess in forming her guest list. There is always another time!

The choice of a menu can be decided according to the season, the availability of certain foodstuffs, tastes —or, the amount of money you feel you can afford for the function.

Another consideration in selecting a menu, particularly for a dinner or brunch, might be your eating arrangement. If snack trays or other informal method of seating arrangement is contemplated, rather than the sturdier card tables or main dining table, it might be well to choose a menu that features an entree that can be eaten with a fork, not needing a knife to cut the meat or the inconvenience of removing bones.

After you have chosen your menu, study it carefully and decide what you may want to do in advance, in steps to suit your convenience. It may be that you will want to select items from the shopping list to purchase days in advance of the party. Make a schedule and a check list of things to do and when to do them in sequence.

The informal buffet dinner and some brunches are often "eaten out of hand" as it were. The assembled guests simply sit down in front of a coffee table, beside an end table, or balance their plates on their laps. Whether you elect a sit-down affair with card tables or a large dining table is a matter of choice, but do plan your way. If you plan an informal seating arrangement, be sure that you do not have too many ornaments on the end tables and on the coffee table. If you plan the card table arrangement, mentally gauge ahead of time where you want to place the tables, chairs and guests. Guests of honor should be seated with the host and hostess, in any event.

It is helpful to plan decorative and furniture rearrangements, when necessary, ahead of time. This would include arranging flowers or greenery in the right containers for height and size to complement table or buffet arrangements, and adjusting furniture to allow walking and seating comfort.

With everything possible done ahead of time, the hostess should be able to relax and enjoy her party, and certainly the guests will be more at ease!

Catering Information

One of the anxieties associated with planning a party is the lack of quantity, size or appropriateness of serving accoutrements.

This problem can easily be solved by renting the needed items from a catering service. Some companies that do food catering rent these items; other companies specialize exclusively in renting party equipment. Usually, the rental charges are quite modest.

Brunches for Six

The increasingly popular brunch, served in the middle of the day on weekends, holidays, or special occasions is usually an informal occasion.

As the name implies, it includes dishes usually served at breakfast combined with foods featured at lunch or late suppers.

No doubt the present-day brunch emanated from the traditional "hunt breakfast" which usually featured an enormous array of hearty dishes for a large number of guests imbued with sharp appetites whetted by a long, arduous, exhilerating ride. A typical hunt breakfast might include an array of food consisting of lamb chops with kidneys, chicken livers, little crisp sausages, ham, bacon, eggs in various forms, assorted exotic fruits and berries, thick cream, preserves, nut breads, hot muffins and scones.

The modern brunch, while not so lavish, certainly can be more different and exciting than the regular breakfast or lunch.

Each of the brunch menus are given in order of their approximate cost—ranging from the least to the most expensive (none, of course, are prohibitively expensive).

BRUNCH MENU $5

Fruit Compote

Steak Stuffed Mushrooms
with
Sour Cream Sauce

French Omelet

Blueberry Muffins

For mushroom fanciers this is it! This brunch is not too difficult to prepare, and the fruit compote as well as the stuffed mushrooms may be prepared ahead.

Shopping Check List

Ground round steak, 1 ½ pounds
Eggs, 1 dozen
Sour cream, 1-pound carton
Butter, ½ pound
Blueberry muffin mix, 1 14-ounce package
Pineapple chunks, 1 1-pound can
Mandarin orange segments, 1 11-ounce can
12 to 14 large, fresh mushrooms, 2-3 inches in diameter
   (1 pound or more)
Onions, dry, 1
Celery, small head
Parsley, 1 bunch
Bananas, 2

(Note: Check your staples, condiments, and spices against what is called for in the recipes. Throughout we have listed only those which might not be standard shelf staples.)

Fruit Compote

1 1-pound can
   pineapple chunks
1 11-ounce can
   mandarin orange
   segments

2 bananas, peeled and
   sliced

Mix fruit and juice and chill. Serve in compote, sherbet, or sauce dishes.

Steak Stuffed Mushrooms
with
Sour Cream Sauce

12 to 14 large fresh
    mushrooms, 2-3
    inches in diameter
    (1 pound or more)
1 ½ pounds ground
    round steak
½ cup each onion and
    celery, chopped very
    fine

⅛ teaspoon pepper
2 teaspoons salt
2 tablespoons A-1
   sauce
1 ½ cups sour cream

Wash mushrooms, remove stems and drain. With knife, remove strips of skin from top of mushrooms at half-inch intervals to make a wheel design, Set aside.

Combine meat, onion, celery, pepper, salt and A-1 sauce; mix well. Divide meat mixture into equal portions for the number of mushrooms and form into patty inside each mushroom cap. Sprinkle mushroom tops with salt. Place meat side down on large flat baking dish. Bake in preheated 450° oven 20 minutes. Remove baking dish from oven, add sour cream to meat juices in bottom of pan, and stir to mix. Return to oven for 3 or 4 minutes until sauce is hot.

Serve on large platter, spooning one-third of sauce around mushrooms. Serve remaining sauce separately. The sauce is delicious on the omelet.

French Omelet

1 dozen eggs	¼ cup butter
½ teaspoon salt	2 tablespoons chopped
⅛ teaspoon pepper	parsley

Beat eggs with salt and pepper just enough to mix whites with yolks. Melt butter in large skillet. Add eggs; cook over medium heat. Keep lifting omelet around edges, tipping pan slightly to allow uncooked portion to flow underneath. When eggs are set but top is still moist, loosen edges and fold one half over the other and slide omelet onto oblong platter. Garnish with chopped parsley or surround with a few sprigs, as desired.

Blueberry Muffins

1 14-ounce package
blueberry muffin
mix

Mix and bake according to package directions.

BRUNCH MENU $5

Minted Strawberry Cup
Quiche Lorraine
Canadian Bacon with Glazed Pineapple
Cranberry Loaf

Quiche Lorraine has been a favorite of the French housewife for generations, and rightly so. Now that frozen pie shells can be readily obtained, preparation time may be cut down considerably. The accompaniments are easily prepared and complement the flavor of the delicate Swiss cheese pie.

13

Shopping Check List

Bacon, ½ pound, sliced
Canadian bacon, ½ to ¾ pound (12 to 14 slices)
Swiss cheese, ½ pound
Milk, rich, 1 quart
Eggs, ½ dozen, large
Butter, ½ pound
Pie shell, 9-inch, frozen
Strawberries, 3 10-ounce packages, frozen, or
   2 baskets, fresh
Pineapple slices, 1 15 ½-ounce can
Cranberry loaf mix, 1 16 ½-ounce package
Brown sugar, 1 pound
Mint extract, small bottle

Minted Strawberry Cup

3 10-ounce packages
   frozen strawberries,
   or 2 baskets, fresh

½ teaspoon mint
   extract

Thaw frozen strawberries. If using fresh strawberries—clean, slice, or leave whole if desired, and sweeten to taste. Add mint extract and mix. Serve chilled in compote or sherbet dishes.

Quiche Lorraine

6 strips bacon, cut
   in halves
1 9-inch frozen pie
   shell, defrosted 15
   minutes
12 thin slices Swiss
   cheese, approximate-
   ly 1 ½ by 3 inches
3 large eggs

2 teaspoons flour
¼ teaspoon each salt
   and powdered
   mustard
   Dash or two of
   cayenne pepper
1 ½ cups rich milk
1 tablespoon melted
   butter

Fry bacon slowly until crisp, draining off fat as it accumulates. Drain on paper toweling. Line unbaked pie shell with bacon and Swiss cheese slices.

Beat together eggs, flour, salt, mustard and cayenne. Add milk and melted butter, mix, and pour over bacon and cheese.

Place cookie sheet in oven and preheat to 375°. Place pie on cookie sheet and bake for 35-40 minutes, or until custard has set (toothpick inserted in center should come out dry).

Cut in 6 wedges, serve on individual plates, or arrange wedges on serving dish, or serve in pie tin placed on appropriate-sized platter.

May be held in oven with heat turned off, door ajar, for 10 to 15 minutes.

Canadian Bacon with Glazed Pineapple

2 tablespoons butter
12 to 14 thin slices Canadian bacon
1 15 ½-ounce can pineapple slices, drained (reserve juice)

⅓ cup of reserved pineapple juice
3 tablespoons brown sugar

Melt butter in large skillet and fry Canadian bacon slices over medium heat, browning slightly on each side. Remove to serving platter. Add drained pineapple slices to skillet, simmer a few minutes, turning once; add pineapple juice and brown sugar. Continue to simmer an additional few minutes until sauce is consistency of syrup.

Arrange Canadian bacon and pineapple slices on platter by either placing bacon in center surrounded by pineapple, or topping each slice of pineapple with a slice or two of bacon. Ladle syrup remaining in pan over all.

Cranberry Loaf

Prepare packaged cranberry loaf mix according to package directions early in the day or the day before; it should be cold to slice well. Butter is all that is needed as an accompaniment.

BRUNCH MENU $5

Grapefruit and Avocado Salad

Crisp Bacon

Scrambled Eggs with Swiss Cheese

Lyonnaise Potatoes

Assorted Hot Rolls

This brunch features a standard combination of bacon, eggs, and fried potatoes. The piquant salad and addition of Swiss cheese to the eggs, plus the onion flavor in the crisp potatoes makes an elegant party version of an old-time favorite.

Shopping Check List

Bacon, 1 pound, sliced
Swiss cheese, 6 slices processed, or ⅓ pound natural
Eggs, 1 dozen, large
Half and half or light cream, ½ pint
Butter, ½ pound
Assorted rolls, 1 dozen
Grapefruit, 2 1-pound cans, segments, or 3 large, fresh
Lettuce, small head
Potatoes, 4 medium
Onions, dry, 1
Avocados, 2
Red garlic wine vinegar, small bottle
Oil, vegetable, 1 pint

Grapefruit and Avocado Salad

Lettuce leaves for garnish

2 1-pound cans grapefruit segments, drained; or 3 large fresh grapefruits, peeled, separated into segments (remove outside membrane from each segment)

2 avocados peeled and cut in half-inch slices lengthwise

2 ½ tablespoons red garlic wine vinegar

½ cup vegetable oil

½ teaspoon each garlic and seasoning salt

¼ teaspoon each paprika and dry mustard

1 teaspoon sugar

Arrange crisp lettuce leaves on individual salad plates. Alternate grapefruit and avocado segments over lettuce and dress with dressing made with the vinegar, oil and seasonings.

Salad may be made one-half to an hour ahead of time and refrigerated. Dressing should be applied when salad is prepared in order to keep avocado from darkening.

Crisp Bacon

1 pound sliced bacon

Lay separated bacon slices in cold large skillet. Cook slowly over low heat. Don't let fat smoke—it will change the flavor. Pour off fat as it accumulates. Press bacon and turn with spatula until golden brown. Drain on paper toweling.

Scrambled Eggs with Swiss Cheese

1 dozen large eggs	6 slices processed
¾ teaspoon salt	Swiss cheese, cut in
Dash or two of	small cubes, or ⅓
pepper	pound natural,
3 tablespoons half and	coarsely grated
half or light cream	3 ¼-inch pats butter

Beat eggs with salt, pepper and cream added, just enough to mix yolks with whites (not to a froth). Add Swiss cheese and stir to mix.

Melt butter in large skillet over low heat; add egg mixture. As the eggs coagulate on the bottom and edges of the pan, pull the solids to the center. Keep moving and blending until eggs are not quite solid and still moist. Remove from heat and stir into a scrambled mixture. Serve at once.

The scrambled eggs may be served on individual plates with bacon portions or on a large warmed serving platter surrounded with the bacon strips.

Lyonnaise Potatoes

⅓ cup vegetable oil	1 teaspoon salt
4 medium-sized	Dash or two of
potatoes, peeled and	pepper
thinly sliced	
1 medium-sized dry	
onion, peeled and	
thinly sliced	

Heat oil in large skillet, add potatoes and onion slices, salt and pepper. Cook over low heat, covering first 10 minutes. Remove cover, turn and cook an additional 10 minutes or more, turning again if necessary, until potatoes are tender and slightly brown. Serve on individual plates or on separate serving dish, as desired.

Broiled Grapefruit

Pancake Omelet
with
Fried Apples and Sour Cream
Little Pig Sausages

This is not only an inexpensive brunch, but happily the soufflé-type omelet, with its topping of fried apples and sour cream, is unusual and truly delicious.

Shopping Check List

Little pig sausages, 1 ½ pounds
Eggs, ½ dozen, large
Sour cream, ½ pint
Butter, ½ pound
Buttermilk, 1 quart
Baking soda, small box
Pancake mix, small box
Brown sugar, 1 pound
Grapefruit, 3 large
Apples, cooking, 6 large

Broiled Grapefruit

3 large grapefruits	**Cinnamon**
6 tablespoons brown sugar	**6 teaspoons butter**

Cut grapefruits in half. With sharp paring knife cut around the edge of each half, remove core, and loosen the sections. Sprinkle 1 tablespoon brown sugar over each half, add a dash or two of cinnamon and dot with butter.

Broil 4 inches from heat about 10 minutes, or until tops are golden brown. No harm is done if grapefruit

19

halves are removed from oven several minutes while omelet is browning under broiler.

Pancake Omelet
with
Fried Apples and Sour Cream
Little Pig Sausages

1 ½ pounds pig sausages	1 cup buttermilk
6 large cooking apples	3 eggs
7 tablespoons butter	1 cup pancake mix
¾ cup brown sugar	½ pint sour cream
½ teaspoon baking soda	

Simmer sausages in large skillet until done and lightly brown but not hard. Drain on paper toweling and place in warm oven. Drain fat from skillet leaving any brown residue in pan.

Peel, core and thinly slice apples. Add 6 tablespoons butter to pan in which sausages were cooked. Fry apples until tender, about 10 minutes, covering last few minutes. When almost done stir in brown sugar.

Dissolve baking soda in buttermilk. Separate the eggs, beat the yolks and add buttermilk. Stir in pancake mix. Beat the egg whites stiff and stir into batter.

Heat 1 tablespoon butter in a 10- or 12-inch frying pan. Pour in batter. Cook over medium heat about three minutes. Place in broiler about 4 inches from heat and continue cooking until top is delicately brown. Test with toothpick (should come out dry) to assure that omelet is done. If not done, lower heat and continue to cook another minute or two.

Turn pancake omelet onto large serving platter. Spread fried apples over top of omelet and cover with sour cream. Cut in serving wedges and surround with sausages.

Cranberry Juice Cocktail

*Sautéed Chicken Livers in Wine Sauce
with Bacon*

Eggs Baked in Tomato Shells

Assorted Small Sweet Rolls

A gourmet treat! And chicken livers are comparatively inexpensive. The Parmesan, basil-flavored tomatoes and eggs make a light and complementary accompaniment.

Shopping Check List

Chicken livers, 2 pounds
Bacon, ½ pound
Eggs, ½ dozen, large
Parmesan cheese, 3 ounces
Butter, ¼ pound
Bread, white, 1 small loaf
Assorted small sweet rolls, 1 dozen
Cranberry juice cocktail, 1 32-ounce bottle
Red dry wine, small bottle
Tomatoes, firm but ripe, 6 medium large (approximately 2 ½ pounds)
Onion, 1
Green bell pepper, 1
Parsley, small bunch

Cranberry Juice Cocktail

1 **32-ounce bottle
cranberry juice
cocktail**

Chill and serve in 6-ounce cocktail glasses.

Sautéed Chicken Livers in Wine Sauce
with Bacon

½ pound sliced bacon,
  diced
4 tablespoons each
  finely chopped onion
  and green bell pepper
2 pounds chicken livers
1 cup flour
  (approximately)

⅛ teaspoon powdered
  thyme
½ teaspoon seasoning
  salt
1 cup red dry wine
½ cup finely chopped
  parsley
6 slices white toast

In large skillet over low heat sauté diced bacon, onion, and bell pepper until bacon is slightly brown. Add the chicken livers, lightly dredged with flour, and let them cook 4 or 5 minutes, tossing them with a fork to brown on all sides (will be still pink around edges). Add thyme, seasoning salt and wine. Simmer for a few minutes, stirring gently. Add chopped parsley. (If sauce becomes quite thick before serving, add a little hot water to thin.)

Serve on individual serving plates over toast which has been cut diagonally in quarters.

Eggs Baked in Tomato Shells

6 firm, ripe tomatoes
  Butter
6 tablespoons grated
  Parmesan cheese
1 teaspoon basil
  leaves, crushed

½ teaspoon each salt
  and seasoning salt
6 large eggs
  Paprika for garnish

Peel tomatoes. This may be done with a paring knife; or put into boiling water for 12 seconds, rinse immediately in cold water to prevent further cooking, then peel off skin; or impale individual tomatoes on cooking fork and slowly rotate over direct high heat on the stove until skin scorches slightly and "splits," then peel off skin. Cut slice off stem ends of tomatoes and scoop out seeds with a spoon leaving a rim of ½ inch or so of pulp. Turn shells upside down on paper toweling to drain.

Arrange shells in buttered baking dish (evening off blossom end slightly if necessary so that shells will not tilt). Mix Parmesan cheese, basil, and salts together and sprinkle inside and top rim of shells, distributing as evenly as possible. Break an egg into each tomato shell, sprinkle tops lightly with salt and paprika, and dot with butter.

Bake in preheated 375° oven 20 to 30 minutes or until the egg whites are set.

Assorted Small Sweet Rolls

**1 dozen assorted small
sweet rolls**

Rolls may be heated if desired for 10 minutes or so in oven along with baked tomatoes.

BRUNCH MENU $7.50

Cranshaw Melon

Oyster Omelet—Crisp Bacon

Potatoes Anna

Tomato Sauce, Piquant

Flaky Biscuits

This omelet dish might be called a "Weight Watcher's Hang Town Fry." However, the buttery, crisp potatoes take it out of this category; but the combination does make an appetizing, not-too-heavy repast.

Oysters, raw 1 ½ dozen medium small, or 2 10-ounce
    jars (raw)
Bacon, 1 pound
Eggs, 1 dozen
Flaky biscuits, 2 4-ounce refrigerated tubes
Chili sauce, 1 12-ounce bottle
Butter, ½ pound
Potatoes, 4 large
Cranshaw melon, 1 6-pound, or 3 12-ounce packages
    frozen melon balls
Green onions, 1 bunch
Parsley, 1 bunch
Lemon, 1

Cranshaw Melon

1 6-pound Cranshaw
   melon, chilled, seeds
   removed, and cut in
   sixths, or 3 12-ounce
   packages frozen
   melon balls

Cranshaw melon makes a wonderful start for this
·brunch but any melon or fruit in season could be substituted.

Oyster Omelet—Crisp Bacon

1 pound sliced bacon
4 tablespoons finely
   chopped parsley (set
   aside 2 tablespoons
   for garnish)
2 tablespoons finely
   chopped green
   onions, including
   tender tops

1 ½ dozen medium small
     raw oysters, or 2
     10-ounce jars (raw)
1 dozen eggs
½ teaspoon salt
   Dash or two of
   pepper
¾ teaspoon Wor-
   cestershire sauce

In two 8- to 10-inch skillets, fry bacon slowly until fairly crisp. Remove and drain on paper toweling. Pour off all but approximately 2 tablespoons fat in each skillet. Add 1 tablespoon each of parsley and green onion to each pan. Drain oysters and divide equally in each skillet. Cook over medium heat, turning oysters once or twice until oysters are plump and edges curled (about 5 minutes).

Beat eggs and season with salt, pepper, and Worcestershire sauce. Spread oysters proportionately around in skillets and pour one-half of egg mixture into each skillet. Cook over medium heat. Keep lifting omelets around edges, tipping pans slightly to allow uncooked portion to flow underneath. Cook until eggs are set but top still moist.

Divide each omelet in thirds and place on individual serving plates. Sprinkle reserved chopped parsley over tops of omelet and surround with bacon slices.

Potatoes Anna

6 cups peeled potatoes, very thinly sliced (about 4 large)	Dash or two of pepper
¾ teaspoon salt	½ cup butter, room temperature

Soak sliced potatoes in cold water for a few minutes, drain and dry on paper toweling. Season with salt and pepper. Generously butter a round baking dish (approximately 2-quart capacity) and arrange a few slices flat on the bottom and sides. Then add a layer of potatoes, spread with 1 tablespoon butter. Repeat, with about five additional layers, and add a final spread of butter on top.

Bake in 425° oven for 40 to 50 minutes, or until potatoes are golden brown on bottom and sides and are soft when tested with a sharp knife. To serve, invert on a serving dish and slip out potatoes.

Tomato Sauce, Piquant

⅔ cup chili sauce
1 tablespoon
lemon juice

1 teaspoon Wor-
cestershire sauce

Mix and serve in small sauceboat for accompaniment to omelet and potatoes.

Flaky Biscuits

2 4-ounce refrigerated
tubes flaky biscuits

The biscuits can be baked as directed along with the Potatoes Anna.

Buffet Dinners for Twelve

The buffet dinner is one of the joys of modern day entertaining. The menu can include a wide variety of epicurean delights, without the host and hostess being encumbered with the details of course service at the dining table! The guest list can be expanded to include more guests than your dining table might afford. The serving platters and dishes can be more varied than is customary at the dining table and be very attractive.

The menus for buffet dinners presented here are designed for ease and comfort in entertaining. Many of the dishes can be prepared a day or two before the event, and most of the hot dishes will not suffer if kept warm for a period of time in a chafing dish or warm oven. In all cases, ease of preparation and availability of all items called for in the recipes, regardless of season or geographical location, are taken into consideration.

Service Arrangement Suggestions

A buffet or long narrow table is ideal for buffet service as it can be placed flat against a wall, allowing more area for guests. However, two small tables can be placed together; or a round, rectangular or hunt-style table may be used.

Plan your table decorations so they can be placed to the wall side of the table. You may use varied china and silver serving platters. Many family treasures in the form of odd bowls and serving dishes may be used if they do not clash with your overall color plan.

Do plan on having a separate small table or tea cart for beverage service. It is thoughtful of a hostess to serve the beverage to guests after they are seated; however, they can serve themselves after depositing their filled dinner plates at the places where they are to eat.

A festive and colorful addition to your table might be a hollowed out eggplant or red cabbage to hold a salad dressing or sour cream accompaniment. Your table will be more attractive if you keep a compatible color scheme in mind. Originality in decorations is fun and adds to the pleasure of the party.

Plan your table service so that guest traffic will move in one direction only. Arrange plates on one end, then the main dishes and accompaniments in a logical order. Place the silverware and napkins so that they will be the last items to be picked up by the guests.

Each of the buffet menus are given in the order of their approximate cost—ranging from the least to the more expensive (none, of course, are prohibitively expensive).

Enchilada Casserole

Baked Chiles Rellenos

Mixed Green Salad
with
Caper Dressing

Marinated Garbanzo and Kidney Beans

Fresh French Bread

A California version of a Mexican dinner without the hours of preparation involved in preparing individual enchiladas and chiles rellenos.

Shopping Check List

Ground chuck, 2 ½ pounds
Cheddar cheese, sharp, 1 pound
Jack cheese, 1 pound
Eggs, 1 dozen, large
Garbanzo beans, 1 15 ½-ounce can
Kidney beans, 1 15 ½-ounce can
Tomato sauce, 4 8-ounce cans
Green chile peppers, whole peeled, 3 4-ounce cans
Black olives, pitted, 1 can
Tortillas, white flour or corn, 1 dozen
Dry onion soup mix, 1 package
Red wine vinegar, small bottle
Chili powder, oregano, and camino spices, small
    container each
Capers, 1 small jar
Onions, dry, 2
Green onions, 1 small bunch
Dry garlic bulbs, 2
Romaine lettuce, 1 head
Iceburg lettuce, 1 head
Tomatoes, 3 or 4

Cucumber, 1
Parsley, 1 bunch
French bread, 2 loaves

Enchilada Casserole

2 medium-sized dry onions, chopped

5 garlic cloves, minced

1 tablespoon vegetable oil

2 ½ pounds ground chuck

2 tablespoons wine vinegar

3 tablespoons chili powder

2 teaspoons salt

½ teaspoon each oregano and camino spice, powdered or crushed

2 teaspoons Worcestershire sauce

1 can pitted black olives

4 8-ounce cans tomato sauce

4 cups water

1 package dry onion soup mix (½ cup)

1 pound sharp Cheddar cheese, coarsely grated

6 tablespoons flour

12 white flour or corn tortillas

In a large skillet, sauté onions and garlic in oil over medium heat for 1 or 2 minutes. Crumble meat over onion, turn heat to high and cook, stirring, 7 to 10 minutes, until slightly brown. Add remaining ingredients except cheese, 1 cup water, flour and tortillas. Simmer meat mixture 20 minutes. Mix the flour with the reserved 1 cup water, add to meat mixture and simmer another 2 or 3 minutes.

Grease large flat casserole (10 x 15 inches, or two 7 x 12 inches) and make layers of tortillas, cut in quarters, meat mixture, and cheese. Bake in preheated 350° oven 20 minutes or until bubbly.

This dish may be prepared early in the day, refrigerated, and then baked. If you do this, increase the baking time to 30 or 35 minutes.

Baked Chiles Rellenos

1 **pound Jack cheese**	8 **large eggs**
3 **4-ounce cans whole peeled green chile peppers**	½ **cup flour**
	1 ½ **teaspoons salt**
	Butter

Cut cheese in rectangles about ½-inch thick by 1-inch long. Remove seeds and cut each chile pepper in 3 or 4 strips lengthwise and wrap each piece of cheese with a strip. Beat the yolks of 8 eggs until very light, fold in the ½ cup flour and salt. Beat the egg whites stiff and combine with the yolks. Butter a large flat baking casserole and pour in half of the batter. Add the cheese cubes, top with remaining batter and bake at 400° until nicely browned and set (approximately 20 minutes).

Note: Remove enchilada casserole when done, increase heat to 400°, bake chile rellenos, and replace enchilada casserole in oven a few minutes before serving.

Mixed Green Salad
with
Caper Dressing

1 **head each romaine and iceburg lettuce**	1 **cucumber, peeled, and cut in thin slices**
3 **tomatoes, peeled, and cut in small wedges**	4 **green onions with tender tops, minced**

Separate the leaves of romaine lettuce, discarding any brown portions or coarse white stem parts. Wash thoroughly under running cold water. Trim and remove core from iceburg lettuce. Tear romaine and iceberg lettuce into fork-size pieces, drain in colander and remove to linen towel or paper toweling and refrigerate. This may be done early in the day.

When ready to serve, place in large salad bowl, add tomatoes, cucumbers and onions, and toss with the following dressing.

Caper Dressing

¾ cup vegetable or olive oil (or half of each)

3 tablespoons each wine vinegar and water

1 large garlic clove, crushed or minced

¾ teaspoon each salt and seasoning salt

⅛ teaspoon pepper

1 ½ teaspoons sugar

3 teaspoons capers with juice

Mix thoroughly or shake in covered jar.

Marinated Garbanzo and Kidney Beans

⅓ cup red wine vinegar

6 tablespoons vegetable or olive oil

1 teaspoon each sugar and salt

½ teaspoon seasoning salt

¼ teaspoon oregano, powdered or crushed

Dash pepper

⅓ cup chopped green onions, including tender green tops

3 tablespoons parsley, chopped

1 15 ½-ounce can each garbanzo and kidney beans, drained

Combine all ingredients except beans and mix. Place drained beans in appropriate-sized bowl and stir in marinade. Marinate several hours, or overnight, stirring occasionally. Serve undrained.

Ham Glazed with Apricot Sauce

Oven Baked Beans

Polish Potato and Apple Salad

Fresh Vegetable Platter

Boston Brown and French Bread

In our version of a traditional menu, we give you a different and delicious variation of potato salad and *easy* baked beans, that are even *better* when baked the day before and reheated!

Shopping Check List

Ham, canned, 5 pounds
Bacon, sliced, ½ pound
Butter, ½ pound
Sour cream, ½ pint
Eggs, ½ dozen, large
Pale sherry wine, small bottle
Red wine vinegar, small bottle
Boston brown bread, 2 cans
Pork and beans, 2 1-pound 12-ounce cans
Apricot nectar, 1 12-ounce can
Molasses, small bottle
Dill seed, small container
Capers, 1 3 ½-ounce jar
Apples, 2 tart
Green bell peppers, 1 or 2
Cucumbers, 2 or 3
Lettuce, 1 head
Lemons, 1 or 2
Onions, dry, 4 or 5
Parsley, 1 bunch
Potatoes, about 4 pounds (red rose or new, if in season)

Tomatoes, 4 or 5
French Bread, 1 loaf

Ham Glazed with Apricot Sauce

Remove gelatin and excess fat from 5-pound canned ham. Place in baking pan and cover with one-half of the following Apricot Sauce. Bake uncovered in 325° oven for 2 hours, basting occasionally. After 1 hour spoon over remainder of sauce. When serving, ladle sauce remaining in pan over sliced ham or serve in a separate bowl. If sauce is too thick, thin with a little hot water.

Apricot Sauce

1 **12-ounce can apricot nectar**
½ **cup brown sugar**
½ **cup sherry**
⅛ **teaspoon each cinnamon and cloves**

1 **tablespoon cornstarch mixed with 2 tablespoons water**

Mix first 4 ingredients together in small saucepan and bring to a boil; thicken with cornstarch mixture.

Oven Baked Beans

2 **1-pound 12-ounce cans pork and beans**
2 **teaspoons prepared mustard**
1 **tablespoon Worcestershire sauce**
2 **tablespoons molasses**
3 **tablespoons catsup**

2 **tablespoons brown sugar**
1 **tablespoon instant onion or one small onion, minced**
½ **teaspoon salt**
4 **slices bacon, diced**

Mix all ingredients in large casserole. Cover and bake in preheated 300° oven for 1 ½ hours. This dish is improved if baked the day before and reheated approximately 30 minutes before serving.

Polish Potato and Apple Salad

8 cups cooked potatoes, cooled, peeled, and sliced ⅛-inch thick (approximately 8 medium-large potatoes)

2 small dry onions, finely chopped

2 tablespoons minced parsley

3 teaspoons salt

1 teaspoon chopped capers

½ teaspoon each dill seed and pepper

2 large eggs, lightly beaten

2 tablespoons lemon juice

1 cup sour cream

4 large hard-cooked eggs, diced

2 tart apples, cored, peeled, and diced

Lettuce

Paprika

Add onion, parsley, salt, capers, dill seed, and pepper to sliced potatoes in mixing bowl. Blend the beaten eggs with the lemon juice, sour cream and hard-cooked eggs. Add to potatoes with diced apple. Mix lightly. Serve on large platter lined with lettuce leaves. Dust top with paprika.

Fresh Vegetable Platter

Arrange alternate rows of peeled sliced tomatoes, cucumbers and sliced onions on a large salad platter. Garnish with bell pepper rings. Salt lightly and drizzle salad oil and red wine vinegar over vegetables (about 4 tablespoons oil and 2 tablespoons vinegar).

BUFFET MENU $11

Tropical Pork Spare Ribs
with
Sweet and Sour Sauce

Walnut-Honey Sweet Potato Balls

Marinated Asparagus and Julienne Carrots

Relish Tray

Assorted Dinner Rolls

Most of the preparation for this satisfying and delicious buffet dinner may be done ahead. The spare ribs and sweet potato balls are cooked at the same temperature and will not suffer if left warm for awhile.

Shopping Check List

Pork spare ribs, 7 pounds
Butter, ½ pound
Vegetable oil, small bottle
White wine vinegar, small bottle
Pale dry sherry, small bottle
Sliced pineapple, 1 8 ½-ounce can
Sweet potatoes, 2 1-pound 13-ounce cans
Honey, small jar
Walnuts, 12 ounces, chopped (can or bag)
Asparagus spears, white or green, 2 1-pound cans
Carrots, julienne strips, 2 1-pound cans
Soy sauce, small bottle
Olives, green or black, 1 can
Garlic, dried, 1 bulb
Green bell pepper, 1 large
Celery, 1 head
Radishes, 2 bunches
Cherry tomatoes, 1 basket

Tropical Pork Spare Ribs
with
Sweet and Sour Sauce

7 pounds pork spare ribs, left in whole sides or halves

½ cup soy sauce
Sweet and Sour Sauce (see following)

Place spare ribs in large flat roasting pan, or broiler pan without the grill, and rub or brush soy sauce over all sides of the ribs.

Bake in 325° oven for 1 ½ hours or until tender and fairly brown. Cut spare ribs into one rib or finger-size portions. Arrange on large serving platter and cover with Sweet and Sour Sauce.

Sweet and Sour Sauce

¾ cup each sugar and white wine vinegar
⅓ cup pale dry sherry
¼ teaspoon each salt and ground ginger
1 large green bell pepper cut into ¼-inch strips

1 8 ½-ounce can of sliced pineapple and juice (cut pineapple slices into half-inch segments)
1 ⅓ tablespoons cornstarch mixed with 3 tablespoons water

Place all of the above ingredients except cornstarch mixture in saucepan; bring to a boil. Add cornstarch. Stir over low heat until thickened and clear (about 5 minutes).

Sauce may be made early in the day and reheated. Spare ribs can be held for a half hour or so, in a warm oven, covered with aluminum foil.

Walnut-Honey Sweet Potato Balls

2 1-pound 13-ounce cans sweet potatoes, drained thoroughly and mashed	4 tablespoons butter, melted
1 ½ teaspoons salt	⅔ cup honey, warmed slightly
⅛ teaspoon pepper	1 ½ cups chopped walnuts

Combine mashed sweet potatoes with salt, pepper and butter; mix well and form into balls slightly larger than a golf ball (about 26). Place on large platter or cookie sheet and refrigerate for 2 hours.

Ladle warmed honey over sweet potato balls; turn to coat. Sprinkle walnuts over and again turn and coat, distributing the chopped walnuts as evenly as possible on all sides, remolding if necessary to round shape. Place on buttered cookie sheet or large flat baking dish and refrigerate for another 2 hours or until ready to bake. Bake in 325° oven for 30 minutes.

Marinated Asparagus and Julienne Carrots

2 1-pound cans asparagus spears, green or white	Italian Dressing Marinade (see following)
2 1-pound cans carrots, julienne strips	

Drain cans of asparagus and carrots and place in individual bowls (suggest flat-type bowl for asparagus). Pour Italian Dressing Marinade over vegetables (half in each bowl) and marinate for several hours or overnight, turning or spooning marinade over vegetables once or twice.

When serving, remove from marinade with slotted spoon and arrange on large platter, either with carrots in the middle surrounded by asparagus; half platter of each; or divided in sections.

Italian Dressing Marinade

½ cup oil
2 tablespoons each
  white wine vinegar
  and water
1 garlic clove, minced
  or crushed

½ teaspoon each salt
  and seasoning salt
⅛ teaspoon pepper
1 teaspoon sugar

Mix thoroughly or shake in covered jar.

Relish Tray

Crisp celery, olives, radishes, cherry tomatoes, or other appropriate accompaniments (not too spicy or hot for this dinner, please!).

BUFFET MENU $12

Boeuf Bourguignonne

Gnocchi au Gratin

Italian Green Beans

Fresh Tomato-Avocado Mold
with
Chive Cottage Cheese

French Rolls

The above menu is a pleasing complementary mixture of French, Italian and American dishes. The mold and beef entree can be prepared in advance, as can part of the "dumpling" casserole.

Shopping Check List

Top round steak, 3 ½ pounds
Chive cottage cheese, 2 pints
Eggs, ½ dozen, large
Butter, 1 pound
French rolls, 1 dozen
Green Goddess salad dressing (optional), 8-ounce bottle
    1 8-ounce bottle
Parmesan cheese, 6 ounces
Burgundy wine, small bottle
Sherry wine, small bottle
Tomato paste, 1 small can
Beef bouillon cubes, 2
Chicken broth, 1 can
Flour, 2 pounds
Gelatin, unflavored, 2 1-tablespoon packets
Italian green beans, frozen, 4 packages
Avocados, 3
Green onions, 1 bunch
Lettuce, 1 head
Mushrooms, fresh, small, ½ pound
Onions, white, small, approximately 30
Parsley, 1 bunch
Potatoes, fresh, 3 pounds; or instant, package for 8
Tomatoes, 5 medium
Cherry tomatoes, 1 basket (optional)

(Note: Check your staples, condiments, and spices against what is called for in these recipes. Throughout we have listed only those which might not be standard shelf staples.)

Boeuf Bourguignonne

3 ½ pounds top round
   steak
¼ cup butter, plus
   2 tablespoons
   vegetable oil
4 tablespoons sherry,
   heated
30 small white onions,
   peeled
½ pound small fresh
   mushrooms, washed
   and cleaned
1 tablespoon tomato
   paste

2 teaspoons Wor-
   cestershire sauce
6 tablespoons flour
2 beef bouillon cubes
   dissolved in 2 cups
   water
2 cups Burgundy wine
1 teaspoon salt
¼ teaspoon pepper
2 tablespoons fresh
   parsley, chopped
¼ teaspoon each
   crushed thyme and
   marjoram

Cut beef in 1 ½-inch squares. Heat butter and oil in Dutch oven or large electric skillet. Brown meat quickly on all sides and remove with slotted spoon to another container. Pour hot sherry over meat. Add onions to pan in which meat was browned and cook about 3 minutes, stirring; add mushrooms and cook for 1 minute longer. Add tomato paste, Worcestershire sauce and flour; stir until smooth. Pour in bouillon mixture and stir until mixture comes to a boil; add ½ cup of the Burgundy wine, salt, pepper, parsley, herbs and beef. Cook over low heat until meat is tender, approximately 2 hours. If serving immediately, add remaining wine 5 or 10 minutes before the dish is finished cooking. If prepared in the morning or the day before, bring mixture to a boil, add wine and simmer a few minutes before serving.

Gnocchi Au Gratin

4 cups cold mashed
  potatoes
1 ½ cups flour
6 egg yolks, beaten
  slightly
2 teaspoons salt

¼ teaspoon pepper
1 teaspoon prepared
  mustard
1 ¼ cups grated
  Parmesan cheese
½ cup butter, melted

Combine all ingredients thoroughly except ¼ cup Parmesan cheese and the butter. Cook in several batches; dumplings should not be crowded. Drop dumpling batter by teaspoonfuls into approximately 2 quarts boiling water seasoned with 1 tablespoon salt. Boil gently until dumplings rise to the surface (approximately 5 minutes); remove with a slotted spoon, draining off as much liquid as possible. Place in a large shallow buttered casserole; keep hot in 350° preheated oven. When all dumplings are boiled, pour butter over top; sprinkle with reserved cheese. Increase oven heat to 500° and bake 15 to 20 minutes until dumplings are golden brown on top.

Note: Mashed potatoes should be prepared early in the day. If instant mix is used, prepare according to package directions, adding butter and salt called for. Package for 8 should make 4 cups.

Italian Green Beans

4 packages frozen
  Italian green
  beans

Cook green beans according to package directions. It is suggested that you use olive oil, half garlic and half seasoning salt, instead of the butter and salt called for; however, this is optional.

Fresh Tomato—Avocado Mold
with
Chive Cottage Cheese

2 cups chicken broth

2 tablespoons unflavored gelatin

3 avocados, peeled and mashed

5 tomatoes, peeled, juice squeezed out gently, and cut in small pieces

3 green onions including tender tops, minced fine

2 tablespoons garlic wine vinegar

½ teaspoon Worcestershire sauce

1 teaspoon salt

½ teaspoon seasoning salt

⅛ teaspoon pepper

2 pints chive cottage cheese
Lettuce for garnish and cherry tomatoes (optional)

Warm 1 cup of the chicken broth and sprinkle gelatin over top, stirring until dissolved, 2 or 3 minutes; remove from heat and add remaining 1 cup broth. Chill until thickened slightly.

Mix remaining ingredients (except chive cottage cheese) and stir into chilled gelatin mixture. Pour into 8-cup mold and refrigerate until firm. Serve on platter garnished with lettuce and cherry tomatoes, if desired.

Chive cottage cheese could be served in center of mold, but would be attractive on a separate oblong serving dish, garnished with parsley and dusted with paprika.

This mold can be served without dressing; however, Green Goddess salad dressing is very complementary and, if used, should be served separately in a small bowl.

*Chicken Breasts
with
Avocado Sauce*

Herbed Spaghetti

Italian Green Beans

*Mixed Green Salad
with
Italian Dressing*

Toasted Garlic French Bread

This comparatively inexpensive dinner is truly out-standing party fare. The chicken breast entree is un-usually delicious and attractive. It is ventured that once you have tried the herbed spaghetti it will be-come one of your favorite dishes.

Shopping Check List

Chicken breasts, whole, large, 7 or 8 (or 14-16 halves)
Parmesan cheese, grated, 3 ounces
Butter, 1 pound
Salad oil, 1 pint
Red wine vinegar, small bottle
Capers, 1 3 ½-ounce bottle
White dry wine, small bottle
Chicken bouillon, 1 cube, or chicken stock base
Tomato sauce, 2 8-ounce cans
Sweet basil, dried, small box
Spaghetti, 1 ½ pounds
French bread, 2 loaves
Italian green beans, frozen, 4 9-ounce packages

Mushrooms, fresh, 12-14 large (approximately ¾ pound)
Parsley, 1 bunch
Avocados, 3
Garlic, 1 bulb
Romaine, red, and iceberg lettuce, 1 head each
Tomatoes, medium, 3
Cucumber, long slender, 1
Green onions, 1 bunch

Chicken Breasts with Avocado Sauce

½ cup grated Parmesan cheese
1 teaspoon salt
2 tablespoons chopped parsley
12-14 large mushrooms (approximately ¾ pound)

7 or 8 large chicken breasts, halved, skinned, and boned
½ cup butter
Avocado Sauce (see following)

Mix Parmesan cheese, salt, and parsley. Clean and remove stems from mushrooms (reserve stems for sauce). Sprinkle Parmesan cheese mixture over insides of chicken breasts. Halve mushroom caps and place 2 halves in center of each chicken breast. Roll up chicken breasts and fasten with small skewers or round toothpicks. The above preparation may be done early in the day, rolls covered with plastic wrap and refrigerated.

Brown chicken in butter in large skillet and place in a baking pan. Cover with Avocado Sauce.

Avocado Sauce

2 8-ounce cans
  tomato sauce
1 cup white dry wine
¼ teaspoon coarsely
  ground black pepper
1 chicken bouillon
  cube or 1 teaspoon
  chicken stock base
1 tablespoon chopped
  parsley

Chopped mushroom
  stems
2 tablespoons each
  cornstarch and water
3 ripe avocados,
  peeled and halved
  lengthwise and cut
  in slices crosswise

In the same skillet in which chicken was browned, combine tomato sauce, wine, pepper, bouillon cube, parsley and mushrooms. Bring to a boil and pour over chicken. Cover chicken and bake in 350° oven for 45 minutes or until chicken is tender.

Place chicken on warm serving platter and re- move toothpicks or skewers. Blend cornstarch with water; stir into sauce in pan. Heat and stir until thick- ened. Add avocado slices; pour sauce over chicken.

Herbed Spaghetti

1 ½ pounds spaghetti
3 tablespoons dried
  sweet basil
2 garlic cloves

½ cup finely minced
  parsley
½ cup butter, melted
¼ cup salad oil

Cook spaghetti according to directions on package. When done, drain in a colander. Return to kettle in which it was cooked.

Crumble sweet basil as finely as possible, using fin- gers or crush with a spoon in small bowl. Crush the garlic with a garlic press or mince fine and add to basil along with parsley, melted butter and salad oil. Toss with spaghetti until basil mixture is thoroughly mixed. Serve in warm flat shallow-type bowl or chafing dish. Spaghetti may be held over low heat for a short time.

Italian Green Beans

**4 9-ounce packages frozen
Italian green beans**

Cook according to package directions. Season to taste.

Mixed Green Salad
with
Italian Dressing

**1 head each romaine,
red and iceberg
lettuce, cleaned,
drained, and cut or
torn in bite-size
pieces
3 medium-sized
tomatoes, peeled
and cut in wedges**

**1 long slender
cucumber, peeled
and sliced thin
4 green onions,
including tender
green tops, chopped
Italian Dressing
(see following)**

Place vegetables in large salad bowl, refrigerate, and mix with the Italian Dressing just before serving.

Italian Dressing

**1 ½ cups salad oil
6 tablespoons each
red wine vinegar
and water
2 garlic cloves, minced
or crushed**

**1 ½ teaspoons each salt
and seasoning salt
⅛ teaspoon coarsely
ground black pepper
1 tablespoon sugar
2 tablespoons capers**

Mix above ingredients thoroughly. An ideal way to mix dressing is to shake in a jar with a tightly-fitting lid.

Toasted Garlic French Bread

2 loaves French bread
½ pound butter, room temperature

2 large garlic cloves, crushed

Make 12 crosswise, slanting cuts spaced evenly in each loaf of bread, but do not cut through bottom crust. Thoroughly mix crushed garlic with butter. Holding the cuts in the bread apart, spread all of the cut surfaces with the butter mixture. Enclose each loaf in foil, leaving top open. Bake in 400° oven 10 or 15 minutes.

BUFFET MENU $18

Paupiettes de Veau
(Veal scallops stuffed with bacon, cheese, and sausage)

Potatoes, Knob Hill

Broccoli Amandine

Pears with Cream Cheese Filling

Clover Leaf Rolls

The stuffed veal rolls are not too difficult to prepare and can be made ahead and reheated. Potatoes, Knob Hill, is a western version of a casserole of mashed potatoes, with sautéed mushrooms, parsley, and chives.

Shopping Check List

Veal steaks, ¼-inch thick and flattened, 12 to 14 slices, approximately 4 x 6 inches each, cut from round or rump, about 4 pounds
Pork sausage, mildly seasoned, 1 pound
Bacon, ½ pound
Swiss cheese, natural, 6 ounces
Cream cheese, 1 8-ounce package

Butter, 1 pound
Half and half cream, ½ pint
Eggs, ½ dozen
Clover leaf rolls, 1 ½ dozen
Wine, dry white, 1 pint
Chicken stock base or bouillon cube
Almonds, roasted, chopped or sliced, 3 ounces
Bartlett pear halves, 2 1-pound 13-ounce cans
Broccoli spears, frozen, 4 10-ounce packages
Chives, frozen, 1 2-ounce carton
Parsley, 1 bunch
Carrots, 2
Onions, dry, 2
Mushrooms, fresh, ½ pound
Potatoes, 4 pounds
Garlic, 1 bulb
Lemon, fresh, 1
Lettuce, 1 head

Paupiettes de Veau

12-14 slices veal round or rump, approximately 4 x 6 inches each, ¼-inch thick and flattened, about 4 pounds

1 pound mildly seasoned pork sausage

6 strips of bacon, cut in half

6 ounces natural Swiss cheese, cut in 12 strips, 2-inches long

½ cup butter

2 medium-sized dry onions, quartered and sliced thin

2 carrots, peeled and sliced thin

2 tablespoons flour

2 cups dry white wine

1 teaspoon chicken stock base or 1 bouillon cube

Spread slices of veal steaks on working surface and divide sausage meat in portions for each piece of veal and pat out over surface of meat. Place a strip of bacon and cheese on each portion. Roll up and tie each portion with string.

Melt butter in large electric skillet or Dutch oven. Brown rolls well on all sides. Remove and add onions and carrots to pan. Simmer until vegetables are fairly limp, about 5 minutes. Stir in flour and simmer another minute or two. Return veal rolls, add wine and chicken stock base or bouillon cube. Cover and cook slowly for 45 to 50 minutes or until tender.

Place rolls on large serving platter and remove strings. Skim off excess fat from sauce and spoon sauce over rolls. If sauce is quite thin, reduce to gravy consistency. *Note:* Can be made a day in advance and reheated.

Potatoes, Knob Hill

4 **pounds potatoes, about 8 or 9 medium size**	2 **egg yolks, beaten**
	¾ **cup half and half cream**
4 ½ **teaspoons salt**	**Pepper**
2 **garlic cloves, peeled**	2 **tablespoons finely minced parsley**
½ **pound fresh mushrooms, cleaned, coarsely chopped**	1 **tablespoon minced chives**
½ **cup butter (½ to be used for mushrooms)**	**Paprika**

Peel and quarter potatoes, boil with 3 teaspoons salt and garlic cloves. While potatoes are cooking, sauté chopped mushrooms in ¼ cup butter for 3 or 4 minutes. When potatoes are tender, drain well and mash with remaining butter. Add 1 ½ teaspoons salt, beaten egg yolks, half and half, dash or two of pepper, minced parsley, chives and sautéed mushrooms. Mix thoroughly.

Place mixture in large baking dish or casserole, dust top lightly with paprika, and bake in 400° oven 20 to 30 minutes or until slightly brown and heated through.

Note: Can be made a few hours in advance and baked before serving. If chilled, baking time will be a little longer.

Broccoli Amandine

4 10-ounce packages
  frozen broccoli
  spears
¼ cup melted butter

1 tablespoon lemon
  juice
¼ cup chopped
  toasted almonds

Cook broccoli according to package directions. Drain and arrange on serving platter. Cover with melted butter mixed with lemon juice and then sprinkle with the chopped almonds.

Pears with Cream Cheese Filling

2 1-pound 13-ounce
  cans Bartlett pear
  halves, drained
  (reserve juice)

1 8-ounce package
  cream cheese,
  room temperature
  Paprika

Add a small amount of pear juice at a time to cream cheese, mixing thoroughly until cheese is the consistency of whipped cream. Fill cavity of each pear half with cream cheese mixture, dust lightly with paprika and arrange on lettuce-lined serving platter.

Clover Leaf Rolls

1 ½ dozen clover leaf rolls

Heat rolls in the oven for a few minutes along with potato casserole. Rolls may be split and buttered before serving or butter may be served separately.

Crab Imperial

Fresh Asparagus

Grapefruit and Avocado Mold

Relish Platter

Assorted Dinner Rolls

Crab Imperial is a rich and satisfying casserole-type entree. The other items on the menu complement the delicate flavor of the crab.

Shopping Check List

Crab meat, 3 pounds fresh, or 7 6 ½-ounce cans
Butter, 1 pound
Eggs, ½ dozen
Mayonnaise, 1 pint
Bread, white, 1 small loaf
Assorted dinner rolls, 2 dozen
Gelatin, unflavored, 2 envelopes
Grapefruit sections, 2 1-pound cans
Grapefruit juice, unsweetened, 1 16-ounce can
Olives, large ripe, 2 1-pound cans
Pimientos, small jar
Pepperoncini salad peppers, 1 jar
Avocados, 2
Cherry tomatoes, 2 baskets, or 4 or 5 regular-sized tomatoes
Onion, dry, 1
Green bell pepper, 1
Parsley, 1 bunch
Asparagus, fresh, 6 pounds, or frozen, 4 10-ounce packages
Celery, 1 bunch
Lettuce, 1 head

Crab Imperial

3 pounds fresh, or
  7 6 ½-ounce cans
  crabmeat
½ cup finely minced
  onion
¼ cup each finely
  minced green
  pepper and parsley
¾ cup butter
1 ½ teaspoons salt

3 teaspoons each dry
  mustard and Wor-
  cestershire sauce
⅛ teaspoon each
  pepper and tabasco
  sauce
6 egg yolks, beaten
1 ½ cups soft bread
  crumbs, heated in
  skillet with 4 table-
  spoons butter

Pick over crabmeat to remove any shell particles and separate into bite-size pieces. (If canned crabmeat is used, drain.) Simmer onion, pepper and parsley in the ¾ cup butter over medium heat until limp (approximately 3 or 4 minutes) and combine with other ingredients except bread crumbs. Mix gently but thoroughly.

Divide into 12 individual baking ramekins or shells, or use one or two flat-type baking dishes (crab mixture should be about 1-inch thick). Top with buttered crumbs.

Bake at 400° for 20 minutes, or until crumbs are golden brown. Large baking dish will take 5 to 10 minutes longer baking time.

Shells or baking dish may be kept warm on flat-type warming unit on buffet or placed on serving tray just before dinner service begins.

Fresh Asparagus

6 pounds fresh
  asparagus, or 4
  10-ounce frozen
  packages

¼ cup melted butter

54

If fresh asparagus is used, wash and snap off tough ends. An ideal way to cook asparagus so the stalks will be tender but the tips not overcooked, is to tie them in bundles and stand on end in large cooking pot in salted boiling water not covering tips. Cover and boil until stalks are tender. Drain carefully, remove strings, and arrange on large serving platter. Drizzle melted butter over the asparagus.

If frozen asparagus is used, cook according to package directions.

Grapefruit and Avocado Mold

2 1-pound cans grapefruit sections
1 16-ounce can un-sweetened grape-fruit juice
2 envelopes (2 table-spoons) unflavored gelatin
⅓ cup sugar

½ teaspoon salt
2 avocadoes, peeled and diced
½ cup celery, diced
¼ cup pimiento, diced
Small bowl of mayonnaise
1 head of lettuce, chilled

Drain canned grapefruit sections, reserving 1 ½ cups liquid. Add 2 cups grapefruit juice, making a total of 3 ½ cups juice. Sprinkle gelatin on top of 1 cup of liquid to soften. Heat remaining 2 ½ cups liquid to just below boiling point. Pour over softened gelatin and stir until dissolved. Add sugar and salt; stir until dissolved. Chill until the consistency of unbeaten egg white. Fold in drained grapefruit sections, avocado, celery and pimiento. Turn into a large mold; chill until firm. Arrange chilled and blot-dried lettuce leaves on large platter; unmold salad in center. Accompany with a small bowl of mayonnaise.

Relish Platter

2 1-pound cans large
   ripe olives
1 jar pepperoncini
   salad peppers

2 baskets cherry
   tomatoes, or 4 or
   5 regular-sized
   tomatoes

Drain olives and peppers. Wash cherry tomatoes. If whole tomatoes are used, peel, quarter, salt lightly, and drizzle with a little oil and vinegar or bottled French dressing. Arrange relishes on divided relish plate or arrange in rows on serving platter.

Cocktail Parties for Fifteen

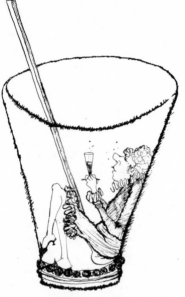

A cocktail party consists of three basic elements—people, drinks and food to enhance the enjoyment of the liquid refreshments. Food is what we're concerned with here—bright, imaginative hors d' oeuvres to delight the palate.

In planning ahead for your cocktail party, it is suggested that you determine the number of guests, then select a menu and the type of drinks to be served. Punches with liquor, or mixed drinks are usually figured on an average of three or four drinks per person. However, it is wise to prepare or have more mix and liquor on hand than this amount.

A buffet arrangement may be used for food service, with a setting of small salad-type plates, forks and napkins. The canapés and relishes can be arranged attractively, and warming units or chafing dishes can be used for the items that should be kept warm.

Each of the cocktail party menus are given in order of their approximate cost—ranging from the least to the more expensive (none, of course, are prohibitively expensive).

COCKTAIL PARTY MENU $10

Onion Flavored Cracker Thins

Chicken Liver Pâté
with
Stuffed Egg Platter

Cream Cheese-Avocado
and
Bacon-Cheese Canapés

Pickled Herring and Onions in Sour Cream
with
Rye Bread Buffet Rounds

Radish Roses and Mixed Olives

This is a combination of party fare that will please guests with a cosmopolitan appetite as well as those who may prefer the milder flavored deviled eggs and canapé spreads.

Shopping Check List

Chicken livers, 1 pound
Bacon, ½ pound
Eggs, 2 dozen
Bacon-cheese spread, 2 6-ounce jars
Cream cheese, 1 8-ounce package
Half and half cream, ½ pint
Butter, ½ pound
Anchovy paste, 1 tube
Pickled herring and onions in sour cream, 2 6-ounce jars
Mayonnaise, 1 small jar
Chives, frozen, 2-ounce carton
Pimientos, sliced, 2-ounce jar
Onion flavored cracker thins, 1 package
Green pimiento stuffed olives, 1 large jar

Black pitted olives, 2 1-pound cans
Sherry wine, small bottle
Rye bread, buffet loaf, sliced, 1
Bread, large square sandwich loaf, 1
Parsley, small bunch
Onion, dry, 1
Apple, 1
Avocado, 1 ripe
Radishes, 3-4 bunches
Garlic bulb, 1

(Note: Check your staples, condiments, and spices against what is called for in the recipes. Throughout we have listed only those which might not be standard shelf staples.)

Chicken Liver Pâte
with
Onion Flavored Cracker Thins

1 **pound chicken livers**
1 **cup half and half cream**
6 **tablespoons butter**
1 **medium-sized dry onion, chopped fine**
1 **apple, peeled, cored, and chopped fine**
½ **garlic clove, chopped fine**
1 **pinch each powdered thyme and marjoram**
½ **teaspoon salt**
¼ **teaspoon pepper**
½ **cup sherry**
1 **package onion flavored cracker thins**

Simmer chicken livers in the light cream for 5 minutes. Drain and reserve broth. Heat butter in medium-sized skillet, add livers, onion, apple and garlic and sauté until golden brown. Cover and simmer an additional 10 minutes over low heat. Add spices, salt and pepper, cream broth and sherry and cook another minute or two. Mix in blender until smooth, or put through a fine sieve. Cool. Round in mold shape in center of large platter and surround with cracker thins.

Stuffed Egg Platter

Place 2 dozen eggs in cold water and bring to a boil; lower heat and simmer 15 minutes. Cool and peel. Halve, remove yolks, 12 each to 2 bowls. Place the white halves on a large platter or two, and reserve in refrigerator while making fillings. Eggs should be prepared several hours before serving and refrigerated so that the stuffing mixtures will firm up.

Deviled Eggs

- 12 **hard-cooked egg yolks**
- 4 **tablespoons each soft butter and mayonnaise**
- 2 **teaspoons prepared mustard**
- 1 **teaspoon seasoning salt**
- ½ **teaspoon salt**
- 2 **tablespoons chopped chives**
- 4 **teaspoons Worcestershire sauce**
- 24 **slices pimiento, approximately 1-inch long**

Put yolks through a fine sieve or mash thoroughly with a fork. Add remainder of ingredients except pimiento strips; beat until very creamy and smooth. Fill 24 halved egg whites. Place strip of pimiento lengthwise on top of each half.

Anchovy Stuffed Eggs

- 12 **hard-cooked egg yolks**
- 4 **tablespoons each soft butter, mayonnaise and anchovy paste**
- 2 **tablespoons finely chopped parsley**

Put yolks through a fine sieve or mash thoroughly with a fork. Add butter, mayonnaise and anchovy paste; mix thoroughly. Fill 24 halved egg whites. Sprinkle chopped parsley over tops.

Cream Cheese-Avocado
and
Bacon-Cheese Canapés

Cut crusts from 1 large loaf of white sliced sandwich bread. Cut each slice with 2 diagonal cuts to make 4 triangles. Use half of the triangles for each of the following spreads.

Cream Cheese-Avocado Spread

1 **8-ounce package cream cheese**
1 **avocado, ripe, pitted and peeled**
2 **tablespoons butter, softened**
1 **pinch each salt and celery salt**

1 **tablespoon chopped chives**
1 **teaspoon Worchestershire sauce**
Green pimiento stuffed olives for garnish

Mash cheese and avocado thoroughly in bowl. Add softened butter, salts, chives and Worcestershire. Beat until smooth. Spread mixture on half of the bread triangles. Garnish each triangle with a slice of pimiento stuffed olive (using a small portion of olives purchased for relish tray).

Bacon-Cheese Spread

2 **6-ounce jars bacon-cheese spread**
½ **pound sliced bacon**

Pitted black olives for garnish

Remove bacon-cheese spread to medium-sized bowl and let soften at room temperature for an hour or two. Fry bacon slices until crisp; drain on paper toweling. Crumble; add to cheese mixture and mix thoroughly. Spread on remaining bread triangles. Garnish each triangle with a slice of pitted black olive (using a small portion of olives purchased for relish tray).

Pickled Herring and Onions in Sour Cream
with
Rye Bread Buffet Rounds

2 6-ounce jars pickled herring and onions in sour cream

1 loaf buffet rye bread, sliced

Remove herring to bowl. Separate herring pieces and cut into serving-size portions (about 1-inch long); return portions to sour cream mixture. Refrigerate until ready to serve. Serve in dish placed in center of large platter and surround with rye bread slices.

Radish Roses and Mixed Olives

3 to 4 bunches radishes
1 large jar pimiento stuffed olives

2 1-pound cans black pitted olives

Clean and trim radishes, leaving about 1 inch of tender green leaves on stem end. With a sharp paring knife cut 5 to 6 thin strips of the peeling from the top to approximately ½ inch of the bottom of each radish to assimilate the petals of a rose. Place radishes in large bowl and cover with cold water. Refrigerate until ready to serve.

Serve olives and radishes in separate serving dishes or in a large divided relish tray.

COCKTAIL PARTY MENU

Cheese Board

Apple Wedges

Smoked Oysters

Liverwurst Spread

Party Rye and French Roll Slices,

Onion Flavored Cocktail Crackers

Relish Tray

Dry Roasted Mixed Nuts

This party could be called a bachelor's delight, or perhaps more appropriately, expediency-type fare for spur of the moment entertaining. There is very little preparation involved and you will find that the interesting, flavorful cheeses and accompaniments will please all tastes.

Shopping Check List

Gjetost, Liederkranz, Fontina, and Muenster cheese,
    8 ounces each
Oysters, smoked, 4 3 ½-ounce cans
Liverwurst spread, 3 4 ¾-ounce cans
Butter, ¼ pound
Rye bread, party type, 1 loaf
French rolls, 6
Cocktail crackers, onion flavored, 1 9 ½-ounce package
Cucumber pickle slices (bread and butter type), 1 1-pint
    6-ounce jar
Pepperoncini (Italian peppers), 1 12-ounce jar
Green olives, 1 9-ounce can
Nuts, mixed, dry roasted, 2 8 ¼-ounce jars
Cocktail toothpicks, 1 1-ounce box
Apples, crisp, eating type, 3
Lemon, 1

Cheese Board

8 ounces each Gjetost,   ¼ pound butter
  Liederkranz, Fontina,
  and Muenster cheese

Let the cheese set out until room temperature and place on a cheeseboard with a small knife or two for slicing. The butter may be placed on the board if it is large enough or served in a butter dish.

Apple Wedges

3 crisp eating apples,   Salt
  chilled
1 tablespoon lemon
  juice

Wash, quarter, remove core from apples, and slice each quarter into 3 or 4 wedges. Arrange on serving dish, salt lightly, and sprinkle with lemon juice over exposed surface of apples (to keep wedges from darkening). Suggest that apples be prepared shortly before serving.

Smoked Oysters

4 3 ½-ounce cans   1 1-ounce box
  smoked oysters   cocktail picks

Drain oysters and place on serving dish, impaling each oyster with a pick or have picks nearby for spearing.

Liverwurst Spread

3 4 ¾-ounce cans liver-
  wurst spread

Mound spread on serving dish and accompany with knife for spreading.

Party Rye and French Roll Slices, Onion Flavored Cocktail Crackers

6 French rolls
1 loaf party
rye bread

1 9 ½-ounce package
onion flavored
cocktail crackers

Slice the French rolls with a sharp knife into ½-inch slices (discarding end portions if you desire). Serve the rye and French roll slices in a bread basket and the crackers in another serving container.

Relish Tray

1 1-pint 6-ounce jar
cucumber pickle slices
(bread and butter
type)

1 12-ounce jar pepperon-
cini (Italian peppers)
1 9-ounce can green
olives

Drain the pickles, peppers, and olives and arrange on a relish tray.

COCKTAIL PARTY MENU $12

Smoked Salmon Canapés
with
Sour Cream and Caper Topping

Chicken Livers and Bacon en Brochette

Cream Puff Shells
with
Surprise Fiesta Filling

California Dip with Potato Chips

Olive and Pickle Tray—Curried Mixed Nuts

The smoked salmon canapé is a contest prize winner of one of the authors. The cream puff shells will be a sure conversation piece, and the chicken liver brochettes have an unusual spicy flavor. California Dip is popular everywhere.

Shopping Check List

Smoked salmon, ½ pound
Chicken livers, 1 pound
Bacon, sliced, 1 pound
Sour cream, 1 ½ pints
Cream cheese, 1 8-ounce package
Parmesan cheese, 1 3-ounce can
Half and half cream, ½ pint
Butter, ½ pound
Eggs, ½ dozen
Olive oil, ½ pint can or bottle
Chicken bouillon, 1 cube
Onion soup mix, 1 package
Party-type crackers, 1 box (not spicy)
Mixed nuts, 1 13-ounce can
Cocktail toothpicks, 1 1-ounce box
Potato chips, 1 large package
Basil leaves, small container
Coriander, powdered, small container
Curry powder, small container
Cayenne pepper, small container
Olives, ripe, chopped, 1 4 ½-ounce can
Green chiles, diced, 1 4-ounce can
Capers, small, 3 ½-ounce jar
Olives, 1 can each, large green and black
Pickles, sweet gherkin, 1 12-ounce jar
Lime, 1 (if not available, 1 lemon)
Onion, dry, 1

Smoked Salmon Canapés
with
Sour Cream and Caper Topping

1 cup sour cream (½ pint)

2 teaspoons capers, drained

½ teaspoon each lime juice and garlic salt

½ teaspoon Worcestershire sauce

½ pound smoked salmon, sliced

1 box party-type crackers (not spicy)

Mix sour cream with capers, lime juice, garlic salt and Worcestershire sauce. Arrange smoked salmon slices on crackers and top with sour cream mixture.

Chicken Livers and Bacon en Brochette

1 pound chicken livers, halved, or cut in thirds if large

3 tablespoons butter

1 tablespoon seasoning salt

1 teaspoon each crushed basil and powdered coriander

½ teaspoon pepper

1 pound sliced bacon Cocktail toothpicks

Sauté livers in butter over medium heat 3 to 5 minutes, turning, until slightly brown. Add seasonings. Mix well. Cool. May be prepared ahead of time and refrigerated.

Roll each liver portion in ⅓ slice of bacon, pinning with pick. Place on broiler rack. A few minutes before ready to serve, broil until bacon is crisp on one side; turn and brown other side. Remove to chafing dish, or hold in warm oven between service.

Note: You might like to broil the livers in two batches if you are entertaining over a period of a few hours.

Cream Puff Shells
with
Surprise Fiesta Filling

Puffs

¾ **cup water**
6 **tablespoons butter**
¾ **cup sifted flour**

3 **large eggs**
Parmesan cheese

Preheat oven to 400°. Heat water and butter to a boil in medium-sized saucepan. Add flour all at once and cook, stirring, until mixture forms a ball that follows spoon around pan. Remove from heat. Add eggs one at a time, beating thoroughly after each addition. Drop by scant teaspoonfuls on ungreased large cookie sheet about 1-inch apart. Should make approximately 36 shells. Sprinkle with Parmesan cheese. Bake for about 30 minutes, until puffed and lightly brown. Cool.

Just before serving, split one side and put a heaping teaspoonful of filling in each puff.

The puffs may be made ahead of time, or even frozen if you desire. If frozen, thaw out the morning of party, so that they will be thoroughly dry before filling.

Surprise Fiesta Filling

1 **8-ounce package cream cheese, room temperature**
1 **chicken bouillon cube, crushed**
1 **tablespoon finely chopped onion**

¼ **cup half and half cream**
½ **cup finely chopped ripe olives**
1 **tablespoon chopped green chiles**

Add crumbled bouillon cube, chopped onion and half and half cream to cream cheese. Mix thoroughly, stirring until crumbled bouillon cube is absorbed. Stir in olives and green chiles.

California Dip

1 pint sour cream
1 package onion
   soup mix

1 large package
   potato chips

Mix sour cream and onion soup mix thoroughly. Chill. Serve in bowl and surround with potato chips for dunking.

Olive and Pickle Relish Tray

1 can each large
   green and black
   olives

1 12-ounce jar
   sweet gherkin
   pickles

Arrange olives and pickles on serving dish or sectioned relish tray. Keep cool until time to serve.

Curried Mixed Nuts

¼ cup olive oil
1 tablespoon each
   curry powder
   and Worcestershire
   sauce

Dash of cayenne
pepper
1 13-ounce can
   mixed nuts

Heat olive oil in a large skillet and add all ingredients except the mixed nuts. Stir and heat until quite hot. Add the nuts; stir until well coated. Remove from heat. Spread on a cookie sheet lined with brown paper (brown paper bag cut to size will do) and bake in 300° oven for 10 minutes. Cool. Nuts should be prepared several days in advance for flavors to permeate. Return nuts to can, cover tightly and refrigerate until ready to serve.

Herbed Meat Balls

Shrimp Pâté Canapés

Bacon and Avocado Dip

Crock Cheese with Brandy
on
Melba Rye Toast Rounds

Vegetable Tray on Mounded Ice

The spicy, moist herbed meat balls need no sauce to enhance their flavor; and the crock cheese, after the flavors "marry" for a few days, becomes light in texture and develops a heady, pungent flavor. Crisped iced vegetables are becoming increasingly popular at cocktail parties.

Shopping Check List

Ground round or chuck, 1 pound
Bacon, lean, ½ pound
Shrimp, broken, 2 4 ½-ounce cans
Eggs, ½ dozen, large
Butter, ½ pound
Parmesan cheese, 1 2-ounce can
Cheddar cheese, sharp, 4 ounces
Camembert cheese, 3 ounces
Kaukauna Klub cheese food, hickory smoked, 1 8-ounce
    crock or Edam, 8 ounces
Cream cheese, 1 3-ounce package
Salad oil, small bottle
Mayonnaise, small jar

Olives, black, colossal, 1 8 ½-ounce can
Olives, green, colossal, 1 8 ½-ounce can
Bread crumbs, dry, 1 6-ounce container
Wheat thins, 1 10 ½-ounce package
Melba rye toast rounds, 2 4-ounce packages
Tortilla chips, 1 10-ounce package
Wine, Burgundy, 1 small bottle
Brandy, ½ pint
Onions, dry, 2 small
Onions, green, 2 bunches
Parsley, 1 bunch
Lemons, 2
Garlic, 1 bulb
Avocadoes, 2 large or 3 medium
Celery, 1 head
Carrots, slender, 1 bunch
Radishes, 2 bunches
Cocktail toothpicks

Herbed Meat Balls

1 pound ground round or chuck steak	1 large egg
¼ cup dry bread crumbs	½ teaspoon each salt and seasoning salt
1 small dry onion, finely chopped	⅛ teaspoon pepper
2 tablespoons parsley, finely chopped	¼ teaspoon each crushed rosemary and oregano
2 medium garlic cloves, crushed or minced	½ teaspoon Worcestershire sauce
4 tablespoons grated Parmesan cheese	3 tablespoons oil
	¼ cup Burgundy wine
	Cocktail toothpicks

Mix all ingredients, except oil and wine, thoroughly in a bowl. Hand mixing seems to be the best method of assuring that all ingredients are completely combined.

Form meat mixture in small balls (about large marble size) and place on a large sheet of foil or plastic wrap.

Heat oil in large skillet and fry meat balls over medium heat until lightly brown on all sides (you may have to fry one-half at a time, removing and reserving on plate until all are browned).

Pour off accumulated fat, add wine, cover, and simmer for 10 to 15 minutes. Serve in chafing dish with cocktail picks available for spearing.

Shrimp Pâté Canapés

2 4 ½-ounce cans broken shrimp
½ cup butter, softened at room temperature
1 teaspoon each English mustard, lemon juice, and Worcestershire sauce

Dash of Tabasco sauce
½ cup finely minced green onions
1 10 ½-ounce package wheat thins
3 tablespoons finely minced parsley

Drain the shrimps, place on paper towel, blot dry, and then chop fine. In medium-sized bowl, mix the butter, mustard, lemon juice, Worcestershire, Tabasco and green onions. Add the chopped shrimp and blend to a paste-like consistency. Chill. The mixture may be made ahead of time and refrigerated. When ready to serve, place generous dabs of shrimp mixture on the wheat thins and sprinkle with minced parsley.

It is recommended that you spread only a portion of the canapés at a time, and augment the platter when necessary, to prevent the wheat thins from becoming soggy.

Bacon and Avocado Dip

½ pound lean bacon
2 large or 3 medium avocados
1 garlic clove
1 ½ teaspoons salt
2 teaspoons lemon juice
¼ teaspoon chili powder

2 teaspoons finely minced dry onion
1 or 2 tablespoons mayonnaise
1 10 ½-ounce package tortilla chips

Fry the bacon slowly until brown and crisp. Place between paper towels to drain and dry. Peel and mash the avocados in a medium-sized, garlic-rubbed bowl. Add the salt, lemon juice, chili powder, and the minced onion. Mix. Crumble the browned bacon and fold into mixture. Put a film of mayonnaise over mixture to keep it from darkening. Stir before transferring to a serving dish. Serve in center of tray or large platter and surround with tortilla chips.

Crock Cheese with Brandy
on
Melba Rye Toast Rounds

4 ounces sharp Cheddar cheese, grated
3 ounces Camembert cheese
1 8-ounce crock hickory smoked Kaukauna Klub cheese food or 8 ounces Edam
1 3-ounce package cream cheese

1 teaspoon dry mustard
¼ teaspoon garlic salt
2 tablespoons salad oil (reserve 1 tablespoon to add to mixture half way through mixing)
½ cup brandy
2 4-ounce packages melba rye toast rounds

Leave the cheeses out at room temperature until softened. In a heavy mixing bowl fork crumble cheeses and mash thoroughly. Mix in the next three ingredients with a heavy spoon or electric mixer. Beat until smooth. Add the remaining tablespoon of oil and mix again to creamy consistency. Now add the brandy slowly, a little at a time, continually beating. Store in covered crock or other covered container in which it may be served. Place crock on plate or tray and surround with rye toast rounds. The flavor of the cheese spread improves on standing and it should be made several days ahead of time.

Vegetable Tray on Mounded Ice

1 **head celery, stalks cleaned and de-threaded**
1 **bunch slender carrots, peeled**
2 **bunches radishes**
2 **bunches green onions, bottoms and a small amount of green tops cut off, and outer casings removed**

1 **8 ½-ounce can black colossal olives, drained**
1 **8 ½-ounce can green colossal olives, drained**
Crushed ice

Cut each stalk of celery in half, then cut into slender strips about ⅓-inch wide. The carrots should be cut into the same size strips, discarding any tough, coarse ends. Carefully pare the skin of the radishes to within a quarter of an inch or so of the stem end in about five sections to create a rose effect, leaving a small amount of green leaves attached to stem. Thoroughly chill the vegetables and olives.

Fill a long, slender serving dish with crushed ice. Place the celery and carrot strips over the top. Surround sides and ends with onions, olives and radishes.

Chicken Livers
with
Water Chestnuts and Bacon

Stuffed Eggs
with
Caviar Topping

Clam Dip with Potato Chips

Caper Topped Artichoke Hearts

Bleu Cheese and Brandy Spread
on Wheat Thins

Cashew Nuts

The broiled chicken liver tidbits are enhanced by the crispness of water chestnuts. Caviar topping adds a "party" touch to the stuffed eggs. Clam dip is enjoyed by everybody, and this version is great!

Shopping Check List

Chicken livers, 1 pound
Bacon, lean sliced, 1 pound
Bleu cheese, 1 8-ounce package
Cream cheese, 1 8-ounce package
Sour cream, 1 8-ounce carton
Eggs, 1 dozen, medium
Butter, ¼ pound
Caviar, black, 1 2-ounce jar
Clams, minced, 1 6 ½-ounce can
Hearts of artichokes, 2 8-ounce cans (drained weight)
Water chestnuts, 1 4 ½-ounce can
Capers, 1 3 ½-ounce jar
Cashew nuts, 1 13 ½-ounce can
Mayonnaise, 1 small jar

Chives, frozen, chopped, 1 2-ounce carton
Brandy, small bottle
Potato chips, 1 12-ounce package
Mustard, Dijon, 1 5-ounce jar
Wheat thins, 1 10 ½-ounce package
Lemon, 1
Cocktail toothpicks, 1 1-ounce box

Chicken Livers
with
Water Chestnuts and Bacon

1 **pound chicken livers**	1 **pound chicken livers**
1 **4 ½-ounce can**	**Salt and pepper**
water chestnuts,	1 **4 ½-ounce can**
each chestnut cut	**Cocktail toothpicks**
in 3 or 4 slices,	
depending upon size	

Cut chicken livers into halves, if small, or in quarters, if large; salt and pepper lightly. Place a piece of chicken liver on a slice of water chestnut and wrap in bacon strip. Use one or two toothpicks to fasten securely. Arrange assembled pieces on two cake racks and place the racks on broiler pan or other large flat baking tin.

Bake in preheated 500° oven for 10 to 12 minutes or until bacon is fairly crisp. The liver pieces do not need to be turned when placed on a rack. If baked without a rack, you will need to turn after 6 to 8 minutes of baking time. Serve hot.

Note: Bacon fat tends to smoke in a hot oven. To eliminate the possibility of smoking up the kitchen when guests are due, it is suggested, if convenient, that you bake the chicken livers a few hours in advance, decreasing baking time 2 or 3 minutes, draining off fat, and reheating under the broiler a few minutes before serving.

Stuffed Eggs
with
Caviar Topping

1 **dozen medium eggs, hard cooked and cooled**	½ **teaspoon salt**
4 **tablespoons each soft butter and mayonnaise**	2 **tablespoons chopped chives**
2 **teaspoons Dijon mustard**	4 **teaspoons Worcestershire sauce**
1 **teaspoon seasoning salt**	1 **2-ounce jar black caviar**
	Mint or parsley

Peel eggs; halve, and remove yolks to a bowl. Place the white halves on large platter and reserve in refrigerator while making filling. Mash yolks thoroughly with a fork. Add remainder of ingredients, except caviar. Beat until very creamy and smooth. Fill the 24 egg white halves. Eggs should be prepared several hours before serving and refrigerated so that the stuffing mixture will firm up.

Just before serving, spread the stuffed egg halves with a thin coating of caviar. Arrange on platter or serving tray garnished with fresh mint or parsley.

Clam Dip with Potato Chips

1 **8-ounce package cream cheese**	1 **teaspoon lemon juice**
1 **6 ½-ounce can minced clams, drained and juice reserved**	¼ **teaspoon each garlic and seasoning salt**
1 **teaspoon Worcestershire sauce**	1 **12-ounce bag potato chips**

Blend cream cheese, drained minced clams, Worcestershire, lemon juice and salts. Add clam juice (approximately 2 or 3 tablespoons) until mixture is about the consistency of whipped cream. A perfect mix should be thin enough so that potato chips won't break when dunked, but thick enough not to dribble. Serve dip in bowl centered on large serving tray, and surround with potato chips.

Caper Topped Artichoke Hearts

2 8-ounce cans
  (drained weight)
  hearts of artichokes

Garlic salt
1 3 ½-ounce jar
  capers

Drain the artichoke hearts, and place on paper toweling to absorb excess moisture. Cut in half, or if large, in quarters. Sprinkle lightly with garlic salt. Drizzle about ¼ teaspoon caper juice over each portion and press 2 or 3 capers in the top. Cover with plastic wrap or foil and chill for a few hours or overnight. Serve in a long slender serving dish. May be impaled with cocktail picks if desired.

Bleu Cheese and Brandy Spread
on Wheat Thins

1 8-ounce package
  bleu cheese
4 tablespoon each
  brandy and sour
  cream
1 tablespoon
  chopped chives

1 tablespoon
  Worcestershire
  sauce
1 10 ½-ounce package
  wheat thins

Crumble cheese in medium-sized mixing bowl. Add brandy, sour cream, chopped chives and Worcestershire sauce. Stir and mix until creamy. Serve in bowl centered on large serving dish, and surround with wheat thins. Accompany with a butter knife for spreading.

Desserts

The following selection of desserts to accompany buffet dinners range from the simple "expediency" type to those "made from scratch." They also range from the light-type dessert, so desirable after a heavy dinner, to the more sumptuous variety enjoyed by many after a not-so-heavy dinner. All of the recipes will serve 12 to 14 generously.

Lime Sherbet with Chocolate Sauce

This frozen dessert is simple to prepare and is attractive and delicious.

2 quarts lime sherbet	1 16-ounce can chocolate syrup

Spoon sherbet into parfait glasses, filling each one-half full. Add a tablespoon of chocolate syrup to each glass; fill with additional sherbet and top with another tablespoon of syrup. Freeze. May be served directly from freezer without any thawing period.

Angel Mousse

This is truly a "heavenly" dessert; light and fluffy with a delicate liqueur flavor. After preparation it should be refrigerated at least 2 hours and may be prepared as much as a day in advance if desired.

6 **eggs, separated**	2 **envelopes (2 table-**
1 **cup sugar**	**spoons) unflavored**
2 **ounces brandy**	**gelatin**
2 **ounces rum**	½ **cup cold water**
1 **pint whipping cream**	**Maraschino cher-**
2 **teaspoons vanilla**	**ries, drained on**
Dash of salt	**paper toweling**

Beat egg yolks until light and lemon colored, add sugar gradually and continue beating until creamy. Add brandy and rum.

Beat egg whites until stiff, but not dry. Whip cream until stiff. Add vanilla and a dash of salt to whipped cream.

Soak gelatin in cold water for 5 minutes. Place over very low heat until thoroughly dissolved. Mix gelatin with egg yolk mixture and fold in, gently but thoroughly, the egg whites and whipped cream. Pour into sherbet glasses and place a maraschino cherry on top of each glass. Chill.

Fruits with Cheese

A dessert of fresh fruit in season with one or two varieties of cheese is easy to prepare and is a favorite of many—especially men.

The fruit selection might include one or several of the following: apples, pears, peaches, nectarines, grapes, kumquats, apricots, and fresh pineapple.

Appropriate cheeses would be: ripe Cheddar, Camembert, Gruyère, Port du Salut, Roquefort, and Stilton. The cheese should be served at room temperature, not cold.

The fruit and cheese may be served in various ways; two suggestions would be: (1) the fruit served whole in a bowl with wedges of cheese on a separate platter, with a fruit knife and dessert dish for each person; or (2) the fruit cut in appropriate wedges or apportioned and served individually with cheese on the dish or passed separately. If desired, serve crackers or small wedges of buttered French bread with the fruit and cheese.

Pineapple Filled Angel Food Cake

The rich, cherry flaked pineapple filling, with the lightness of angel food cake, makes an attractive, delicious and not-too-heavy dessert.

2 eggs, separated
¼ cup sugar
2 tablespoons pineapple syrup
½ cup butter, room temperature
¾ cup powdered sugar
¾ cup thoroughly drained crushed pineapple (reserve 2 tablespoons syrup)
2 tablespoons chopped maraschino cherries

1 10-inch tube angel food cake (packaged cake is fine)
1 pint whipping cream (slightly sweetened when whipped) or 4 cups whipped packaged topping mix (4 ¼-ounce package)

Beat egg yolks and gradually add the ¼ cup sugar, beating until mixture is thick and lemon colored. Add pineapple syrup and cook over hot water, or in small heavy saucepan, over low heat, stirring constantly until thickened. Cool.

Cream butter until fluffy; gradually add powdered sugar and beat until mixture is very light. Stir in cooled egg mixture and blend well. Beat egg whites until stiff and fold into creamed mixture. Carefully fold in well-drained pineapple and cherries. Cut cake crosswise into four layers, using a long, slender sharp knife. Spread filling between each layer. Chill overnight.

An hour or two before serving, cover top and sides with topping of your choice.

Pumpkin Chiffon Cake

A very light and delicious cake. The pumpkin and spice flavor is reminiscent of pumpkin pie with all of the satisfaction but without the heaviness.

2 cups sifted cake flour	**½ cup salad oil**
1 ½ cups sugar	**8 eggs, separated**
3 teaspoons baking powder	**½ cup water**
	¾ cup canned pumpkin
1 teaspoon each salt and cinnamon	**½ teaspoon cream of tartar**
½ teaspoon each cloves and nutmeg	**Powdered sugar**

Sift dry ingredients (including granulated sugar) into a bowl. Make well in center. Add salad oil, egg yolks, water and pumpkin. Beat until satin smooth.

In a large bowl, beat egg whites and cream of tartar until stiff peak stage. Pour egg yolk batter in thin stream over entire surface of whites. Gently fold to blend until all batter is thoroughly mixed with egg whites.

Pour into ungreased 10-inch tube pan and bake in a preheated 325° oven for 55 minutes. Increase temperature to 350° and bake 10 minutes longer. Invert and remove when cold. Sprinkle top of cake with powdered sugar.

Husband's Cake

An old-time recipe with an unusual name, which is appropriate in that it never fails to please the male guests.

¾ cup butter, softened

1 ½ cups sugar

3 cups flour

3 teaspoons baking powder

2 teaspoons each ground cinnamon and nutmeg

1 ¼ teaspoons ground cloves

1 teaspoon baking soda

¾ teaspoon salt

1 cup condensed tomato soup combined with ¾ cup water

1 ½ cups plumped seedless raisins (see note below)

1 ½ cups chopped walnuts

Preheat oven to 350°. In a mixing bowl cream the butter and sugar until as smooth as possible. Sift together the flour, baking powder, spices, baking soda and salt. Add the sifted dry ingredients to the creamed mixture alternately with the soup mixture, beginning and ending with the dry ingredients. Beat the batter until it is smooth after each addition. Quickly stir in the plumped raisins and walnuts. (To plump raisins, pour hot water over them, let stand 5 minutes, drain thoroughly and blot dry on paper toweling.)

Turn the batter into a well oiled 10-inch tube pan and bake for about an hour or until it tests done. Let it cool in the pan for about 10 minutes, turn out on a wire rack, and let it cool completely. Ice the cake with the following frosting.

Cheese Fondant Icing

Beat 6 ounces soft cream cheese until it is light and fluffy. Beat in 1 egg yolk, 1 teaspoon vanilla and a pinch of salt. Gradually beat in 3 cups sifted confectioners' sugar, or enough to make the icing easy to spread, and beat the icing until it is smooth.

Pears Amontillado

One generally thinks of tarragon as a herb to be used with salads or dressings. Suprisingly, combined with the wine and pear flavor, it adds a marvelous zest to an otherwise mild dessert.

24 pear halves, fresh (peeled and cored), or canned (drained)

4 tablespoons (¼ cup) brown sugar

8 tablespoons Amontillado sherry or Almaden's golden sherry (½ cup)

1 tablespoon dried tarragon leaves

Preheat oven to 250°. Place pear halves cut side up in large flat baking pan. Sprinkle ½ teaspoon brown sugar in core cavity of each pear half. Carefully drizzle 1 teaspoon sherry and then sprinkle ⅛ teaspoon tarragon over the surface of each half.

Cover with aluminum foil. Do not seal. Bake about 15 to 20 minutes, or until warm. May be held in warm oven until ready to serve. Serve two halves per portion in dessert dishes.

Strawberry Mint Parfait

This dessert is delightful and comforting after any dinner you might choose.

2 quarts vanilla ice cream, softened enough to mix

1 cup crème de menthe

2 16-ounce packages frozen strawberry halves, or 2 baskets fresh

¼ cup butter

½ cup brandy

Mix the softened ice cream with the crème de menthe. Spoon the mixture into 12 to 14 parfait glasses up to about 1 ½ inches of the top. Place glasses on tray and freeze. The ice cream mix may be prepared several hours or a day in advance.

Defrost frozen berries. If fresh are used, clean, halve, and mix with ½ cup sugar. Melt butter in saucepan, add brandy, and simmer a minute or two. Add berries with juice and heat until berries are slightly warm. May be prepared in advance and warmed slightly before serving. Spoon strawberries over ice cream just before serving.

Frosty Raspberry Pie

This is an elegant "all season" refrigerated pie. Strawberries may be substituted for the raspberries.

4 **10-ounce packages whole frozen raspberries**

48 **large marshmallows (approximately 12 ounces)**

1 **pint whipping cream**

2 **9-inch graham cracker pie shells, chilled**

Defrost raspberries, drain well, and reserve 1 cup juice. Place the 1 cup juice in saucepan with marshmallows. Heat until marshmallows are completely dissolved. Cool to room temperature.

Whip cream until very stiff and fold into marshmallow mixture. Fold in berries carefully, mixing well until mixture is an even pink color. Pour into chilled pie shells. Refrigerate at least 3 to 4 hours before serving.

Beverages

When entertaining guests a host generally has a set pattern of drinks he likes to serve before, during and after dinner; and the general trend for serving drinks at cocktail parties is to let the guest make the choice. There are times, however, when a change of pace is interesting.

With this in mind, here are a few of the drinks that are universal favorites, and a few that are unusual or new innovations gaining popularity. Included also is a section on wines to aid the host in making an appropriate selection for any occasion.

Note: Each drink recipe serves one.

Bullshot

1 ½ ounces vodka	3 ounces beef bouillon, undiluted

Pour over ice in an old-fashioned glass.

Bloody Mary

1 ½ ounces vodka
  3 ounces tomato
    juice
 ½ ounce lemon
    juice

Dash Worcester-
shire sauce
Dash of salt
and pepper

Mix the above ingredients for the desired amount of servings in a large pitcher. Chill and serve in 8-ounce glasses.

Salty Dog

1 ½ ounces vodka   1 ½ ounces grapefruit
    juice

Shake with cracked ice. Rub rim of old-fashioned glass with rind of grapefruit, lime, or lemon. Dip rim in salt. Pour and serve.

Aquavit Cooler

1 ½ ounces aquavit   Twist of lemon peel
  Club soda

Pour aquavit over ice in old-fashioned glass. Fill with soda and add a twist of lemon peel. This liquor is a product of Scandinavia, is as clear as vodka, and has an unusual peach-pit flavor.

Margarita

1 ounce tequila
1 ounce Cointreau
  or Triple Sec

1 ounce lime or
  lemon juice (or
  less, depending
  on sharpness desired

Shake well with crushed ice. Rub rim of 4-ounce cocktail glass with rind of lime or lemon. Dip rim in salt. Strain into glass and serve.

Vermouth Cassis

1 ounce Crème de Cassis   Club soda
2 ounces dry French vermouth

Stir Crème de Cassis and vermouth with ice in old-fashioned glass. Fill with soda and stir again, gently.

Irish Coffee

1 ½ ounces   Strong, very hot
    Irish whiskey   coffee
1 or 2 teaspoons   1 tablespoon
    sugar   whipped cream

Pour the whiskey in a coffee cup or Irish coffee glass. Add 1 or 2 teaspoons sugar and fill with coffee. Stir to completely dissolve sugar. Float whipped cream on top. Do not stir again; drink through floating cream.

Wines

Wines come in five main categories:

Appetizer wines: Sherry (pale, cocktail, or dry); vermouth; and flavored wines (natural fruit and berry flavors added).

    Good with: hors d'oeuvres or snacks. Serve chilled.

Red dinner wines: Burgundy (robust); Pinot Noir (soft and velvety); Gamay Beaujolais (lighter in body and color); claret and similar types (Cabernet Sauvignon, Zinfandel, Grignolino).

    Good with: beef roasts, pot roasts, steaks, heavy cheese or Spanish omelets, pasta, venison, and duck. Serve at cool room temperature in 6- to 9-ounce glasses.

VIN — SÉLECTIONNÉ

White dinner wines: Sauterne; Semillon; Sauvignon Blanc; Rhine wine and similar types (Riesling, Traminer, Sylvaner); Chablis and similar types (Pinot Blanc, Pinot Chardonnay, White Pinot); and Vin Rosé.

Good with: seafood, chicken, and light omelets. Chill and serve in 6- to 9-ounce glasses.

Dessert wines: Port, Tokay, Muscatel, Angelica, cream (sweet) sherry. Port comes in deep red, pale gold or tawny. The red is usually heavier-bodied. All of the above are fruity in flavor, sweet to medium sweet. The muscatel has the pronounced flavor of muscat grapes; the Angelica is amber-colored and very sweet, resembling white port.

Good with: fruits, cookies, nuts or cheeses, or combinations. Serve chilled slightly or at cool room temperature in 2 ½- to 4-ounce glasses.

Sparkling wines: Champagne, white or pink, ranging from brut (very dry) to sec (semi-dry) and doux (sweet); sparkling Burgundy; and Crackling Rosé.

Good with: appetizers, main courses, and desserts. Especially fine for festive "special occasion" punches. Serve the sparkling wine well chilled, in 5- to 9-ounce glasses.

INDEX

A

Anchovy stuffed eggs, 60
Angel mousse, 81
Appetizer wines, 90
Apple and potato salad,
    Polish, 39
Apple wedges, 65
Apricot sauce, 35
Aquavit cooler, 89
Artichoke hearts, caper
    topped, 79
Asparagus and julienne
    carrots, marinated, 39
Asparagus, fresh, 54
Assorted small sweet rolls, 23
Avocado, grapefruit
    mold, 55
Avocado sauce, 47

B

Bacon and avocado dip, 74

Bacon and water chestnuts,
    with chicken livers, 77
Bacon en brochette, with
    chicken livers, 68
Bacon-cheese spread, 61
Bacon, crisp, 17
Bacon with chicken livers,
    sautéed in wine sauce, 22
Baked chiles rellenos, 32
Beans, oven baked, 35
Beverages, 88-92
Biscuits, flaky, 26
Bleu cheese and brandy
    spread on wheat thins, 79
Bloody Mary, 89
Blueberry muffins, 13
Boeuf bourguignonne, 42
Broccoli amandine, 52
Broiled grapefruit, 19
Brunches, 9-26
Buffet dinners, 27-56

Buffet service suggestions, 28
Bullshot, 88

C
California dip, 70
Canadian bacon with glazed
    pineapple, 15
Caper dressing, 33
Caper topped artichoke
    hearts, 79
Carrots, julienne, and
    asparagus, marinated, 39
Catering information, 8
Caviar topped stuffed
    eggs, 78
Cheese board, 65
Cheese fondant icing, 84
Chicken breasts with
    avocado sauce, 46
Chicken liver pâté with
    onion flavored cracker
    thins, 59
Chicken livers and bacon
    en brochette, 68
Chicken livers, sautéed, in
    wine sauce with bacon, 22
Chicken livers with water
    chestnuts and bacon, 77
Chiles rellenos, baked, 32
Clam dip with potato
    chips, 78
Clover leaf rolls, 52
Cocktail parties, 57-79
Cocktail party planning, 57
Crab imperial, 54
Cranberry loaf, 16
Cranberry juice cocktail, 21
Cranshaw melon, 24
Cream cheese-avocado and
    bacon-cheese canapes, 61
Cream cheese-avocado
    spread, 61

Cream puff shells with sur-
    prise fiesta filling, 69
Crisp bacon, 17
Crock cheese with brandy
    on melba rye toast
    rounds, 74
Curried mixed nuts, 70

D
Desserts, 80-86
Desserts wines, 92
Deviled eggs, 60
Dinner wines, 90-92

E
Eggs:
    anchovy stuffed, 60
    deviled, 60
    stuffed, with caviar
        topping, 78
Eggs baked in tomato
    shells, 22
Enchilada casserole, 31

F
Flaky biscuits, 26
French bread, toasted
    garlic, 49
French omelet, 13
Fresh asparagus, 54
Fresh tomato-avocado
    mold with chive cottage
    cheese, 44
Fresh vegetable platter, 36
Frosty raspberry pie, 86
Fruit compote, 12
Fruits with cheese, 81

G
Garbanzo and kidney beans,
    marinated, 33
Gnocchi au gratin, 43

Grapefruit and avocado
mold, 55
Grapefruit and avocado
salad, 17
Grapefruit, broiled, 19
Green beans, Italian, 43, 48

H
Ham glazed with apricot
sauce, 35
Herbed meat balls, 72
Herbed spaghetti, 47
Herring, pickled, and onions
in sour cream with rye
bread buffet rounds, 62
Husband's cake, 84

I
Iced vegetables, 75
Irish coffee, 90
Italian dressing, 48
Italian dressing mari-
nade, 40
Italian green beans, 43, 48

K
Kidney and garbanzo beans,
marinated, 33

L
Lime sherbet, 80
Liverwurst spread, 65
Lyonnaise potatoes, 18

M
Margarita, 89
Marinated asparagus and
julienne carrots, 39
Marinated garbanzo and
kidney beans, 33
Meat balls, herbed, 72
Melon, Cranshaw, 24

Minted strawberry cup, 14
Mixed green salad with
caper dressing, 32
Mixed green salad with
Italian dressing, 48
Mushrooms, steak stuffed,
with sour cream sauce, 12

O
Olive and pickle relish
tray, 70
Omelet:
French, 13
oyster, 24
pancake, 20
Oven baked beans, 35
Oyster omelet-crisp
bacon, 24
Oysters, smoked, 65

P
Pancake omelet with fried
apples and sour cream
(little pig sausages), 20
Party planning, 7-8
Party rye and French roll
slices, onion flavored
cocktail crackers, 66
Paupiettes de veau, 50
Pears Amontillado, 85
Pears with cream cheese
filling, 52
Pickled herring and onions
in sour cream with rye
bread buffets rounds, 62
Pig sausages, 20
Pineapple filled angel food
cake, 82
Polish potato and apple
salad, 39
Potato and apple salad,
Polish, 39

Potatoes:
  Anna, 25
  Knob Hill, 51
  Lyonnaise, 18
Pumpkin chiffon cake, 83

Q
Quiche Lorraine, 14

R
Radish roses and mixed
  olives, 62
Raspberry pie, frosty, 86
Red dinner wines, 90
Relish platter, 56
Relish tray, 40, 66

S
Salmon canapés, smoked,
  with sour cream and
    caper topping, 68
Salty dog, 89
Sausages, pig, little, 20
Sautéed chicken livers in
  wine sauce with bacon, 22
Scrambled eggs with Swiss
  cheese, 18
Shrimp pâté canapés, 73
Smoked oysters, 65
Smoked salmon canapés
  with sour cream and
    caper topping, 68
Spaghetti, herbed, 47
Spare ribs, tropical pork,
  with sweet and sour
    sauce, 38
Sparkling wines, 92
Steak stuffed mushrooms
  with sour cream sauce, 12

Strawberry cup, minted, 14
Strawberry mint parfait, 85
Stuffed egg platter, 60
Stuffed eggs with caviar
  topping, 78
Surprise fiesta filling, 69
Sweet and sour sauce, 38
Sweet potato balls, walnut-
  honey, 39
Swiss cheese, with scram-
  bled eggs, 18

T
Toasted garlic French
  bread, 49
Tomato-avocado mold,
  fresh, with chive cottage
    cheese, 44
Tomato sauce, piquant, 26
Tomato shells, eggs
  baked in, 22
Tropical pork spare ribs
  with sweet and sour
    sauce, 38

V
Veal, paupiettes, 50
Vegetable tray on mounded
  ice, 75
Vermouth cassis, 90

W
Walnut-honey sweet
  potato balls, 39
White dinner wines, 92
Wines, 90-92